Milly, Molly and Daffodil

"We may look different but we feel the same."

Milly and Molly sat cross-legged among a flutter of blue and yellow budgerigars.

The bright blue one caught Milly and Molly's attention.

He could stand on his head.
"Look at him," cried Milly.

His cartwheels were perfect.
"Watch him now," squealed Molly.

And his somersault was second to none.
"He's mad," giggled Milly.

He could swing by one leg from his perch.
"He's a clown," chuckled Molly.

And he taught the other birds to play football with a pebble. "He's awesome," sighed Milly and Molly together.

"Could we please have that one?"

"There you are," said the kind man in green overalls with feathers in his hair. "His name is Billy Boy."

Milly and Molly took Billy Boy home and stood back to watch his antics.

But Billy Boy seemed to have forgotten how to stand on his head and do cartwheels. A somersault was out of the question.

"Come on, Billy Boy. You can play football with a pebble," coaxed Milly and Molly gently. But Billy Boy would not budge. He was miserable.

The kind man in green overalls with feathers in his hair also had a problem.

"Come on, Daffodil. You used to love watching the football," he coaxed gently.
But Daffodil would not budge. She was miserable.

Milly and Molly took Billy Boy back to the kind man in green overalls with feathers in his hair.

Well... Billy Boy did his antics one after the other and slipped into the football game without an invitation.

"I don't see a problem," said the kind man in green overalls with feathers in his hair. "Perhaps you'd like to choose another one."

Daffodil hopped up and down the sideline in a frenzy of yellow feathers.

"Could we please have that one?"

"Oh no, not that one!" pleaded the kind man in green overalls with feathers in his hair.
"I think Billy Boy and Daffodil are friends and need to be together."

Milly and Molly sat cross-legged among a flutter of blue and yellow budgerigars.

The pale blue one caught Milly and Molly's attention. He stood quietly on his own. "Could we please have that one?"

"Yes, you can have that one," said the kind man in green overalls with feathers in his hair. "I think he needs a friend."